Welsh Airs

Welsh Airs

R.S. Thomas

SEREN BOOKS

SEREN BOOKS is the book imprint of
Poetry Wales Press Ltd.
Andmar House, Tondu Road, Bridgend, Mid Glamorgan

© R.S. Thomas, 1987

Reprinted 1993

British Library Cataloguing in Publication Data

Thomas, R.S.
Welsh airs.
I. Title
821'.914   PR6039.H618
ISBN 0-907476-75-9

Seren Books works with the financial assistance of the
Welsh Arts Council

Printed in 10 point Erhardt
by The Cromwell Press, Melksham

Contents

Welsh History	9
Border Blues	10
On Hearing a Welshman Speak	15
Expatriates	16
Hyddgen	17
A Line from St. David's	18
Welsh	19
Afforestation	20
Welcome	21
A Country	22
A Lecturer	23
The Patriot	24
Looking at Sheep	25
Hafod Lom	26
The Provincial	27
A Welshman at St. James's Park	28
Schoonermen	29
Sir Gelli Meurig	30
Traeth Maelgwn	31
Llanrhaeadr-ym-Mochnant	32
Resort	33
Welcome to Wales	34
Loyalties	35
Alma Mater	36
Toast	37
Drowning	38
Gwalia	39
The Parlour	40
Welsh Village	41
Welsman's Epitaph	42
A Land	43
Saunders Lewis	44
The Cause	45
Dic Aberdaron	46
Dead Worthies	47
Waiting	48
Deprivation	49
Fugue for Ann Griffiths	50

Acknowledgements

We are grateful to William Collins Ltd for permission to reprint certain poems from *Song at the Year's Turning, Poetry for Supper, Tares, The Bread of Truth, Pieta, Not That He Brought Flowers*. 'Fugue for Ann Griffiths' appeared in *Planet*.

Welsh Airs

Welsh History

We were a people taut for war; the hills
Were no harder, the thin grass
Clothed them more warmly than the coarse
Shirts our small bones.
We fought, and were always in retreat,
Like snow thawing upon the slopes
Of Mynydd Mawr; and yet the stranger
Never found our ultimate stand
In the thick woods, declaiming verse
To the sharp prompting of the harp.

Our kings died, or they were slain
By the old treachery at the ford.
Our bards perished, driven from the halls
Of nobles by the thorn and bramble.

We were a people bred on legends,
Warming our hands at the red past.
The great were ashamed of our loose rags
Clinging stubbornly to the proud tree
Of blood and birth; our lean bellies
And mud houses were a proof
Of our ineptitude for life.

We were a people wasting ourselves
In fruitless battles for our masters,
In lands to which we had no claim,
With men for whom we felt no hatred.

We were a people, and are so yet,
When we have finished quarrelling for crumbs
Under the table, or gnawing the bones
Of a dead culture, we will arise,
Armed, but not in the old way.

Border Blues

All along the border the winds blow
Eastward from Wales, and the rivers flow
Eastward from Wales with the roads and the railways,
Reversing the path of the old migrations.
And the winds say: It is April, bringing scents
Of dead heroes and dead saints.
But the rivers are surly with brown water
Running amok, and the men to tame them
Are walking the streets of a far town.

Spring is here and the birds are singing;
Spring is here and the bells are ringing
In country churches, but not for a bride.
The sexton breaks the unleavened earth
Over the grave.
       Are there none to marry?
There is still an Olwen teasing a smile
Of bright flowers out of the grass,
Olwen in nylons. Quick, quick,
Marry her someone. But Arthur leers
And turns again to the cramped kitchen
Where the old mother sits with her sons and daughters
At the round table. Ysbaddaden Penkawr's
Cunning was childish measured with hers.

*

I was going up the road and Beuno beside me
Talking in Latin and old Welsh,
When a volley of voices struck us; I turned,
But Beuno had vanished, and in his place
There stood the ladies from the council houses:
Blue eyes and Birmingham yellow
Hair, and the ritual murder of vowels.

Excuse me, I said, I have an appointment
On the high moors; it's the first of May

And I must go the way of my fathers
Despite the loneli — you might say rudeness.

Sheep song round me in the strong light;
The ancient traffic of glad birds
Returning to breed in the green sphagnum --
What am I doing up here alone
But paying homage to a bleak, stone
Monument to an evicted people?
Go back, go back: from the rough heather
The grouse repels me, and with slow step
I turn to go, but down not back.

*

Eryr Pengwern, penngarn llwyt heno...
We still come in by the Welsh gate, but it's a long way
To Shrewsbury now from the Welsh border.
There's the train, of course, but I like the 'buses;
We go each Christmas to the pantomime:
It was 'The Babes' this year, all about nature.
On the way back, when we reached the hills, --
All black they were with a trimming of stars --
Some of the old ones got sentimental,
Singing Pantycelyn; but we soon drowned them;
It's funny, these new tunes are easy to learn.
We reached home at last, but diawl I was tired.
And to think that my grand-dad walked it each year,
Scythe on shoulder to mow the hay,
And his own waiting when he got back.

*

*Mi sydd fachgen ifanc, ffôl
Yn byw yn ôl fy ffansi...*
Riding on a tractor,
Whistling tunes

From the world's dance-halls;
Dreaming of the girl, Ceridwen,
With the red lips,
And red nails.
Coming in late,
Rising early
To flog the carcase
Of the brute earth;
A lad of the 'fifties,
Gay, tough,
I sit, as my fathers have done,
In the back pews on Sundays
And have fun.

*

Going by the long way round the hedges;
Speaking to no-one, looking north
At every corner, she comes from the wise man.
Five lengths of yarn from palm to elbow
Wound round the throat, then measured again
Till the yarn shrinks, a cure for jaundice.

Hush, not a word. When we've finished milking
And the stars are quiet, we'll get out the car
And go to Llangurig; the mare's bewitched
Down in the pasture, letting feg
Tarnish the mirror of bright grass.

*

Six drops in a bottle,
And an old rhyme
Scratched on a slate
With stone pencil:
Abracadabra
Count three, count nine;

Bury it in your neighbour's field
At bed-time.

*

As I was saying, I don't hold with war
Myself, but when you join your unit
Send me some of your brass buttons
And I'll have a shot at the old hare
In the top meadow, for the black cow
Is a pint short each morning now.

Be careful, mind where you're going.
These headlights dazzle, their bright blade
Reaps us a rich harvest of shadow.
But when they have gone, it is darker still,
And the vixen moves under the hill
With a new boldness, fretting her lust
To rawness on the unchristened grass.
It's easy to stray from the main road
And find yourself at the old *domen*.
I once heard footsteps in the leaves,
And saw men hiding behind the trunks
Of the trees. I never went there again,
Though that was at night, and the night is different.

The day divides us, but at night
We meet in the inn and warm our hearts
At the red beer with yarn and song;
Despite our speech we are not English,
And our wit is as sharp as an axe yet,
Finding the bone beneath the skin
And the soft marrow in the bone.
We are not English...*Ni bydd diwedd
Byth ar sŵn y delyn aur.*
Though the strings are broken, and time sets
The barbed wire in their place,

The tune endures; on the cracked screen
Of life our shadows are large still
In history's fierce afterglow.

On Hearing a Welshman Speak

And as he speaks time turns,
The swift years revolve
Backwards. There Goronwy comes
Again to his own shore.
Now in a mountain parish
The words leave the Book
To swarm in the honeyed mind
Of Morgan. Glyn Dŵr stands
And sees the flames fall back
Like waves from the charred timbers
Before taking his place
Behind the harp's slack bars
From which the singer called him.
Look, in this resinous church,
As the long prayers are wound
Once more on the priest's tongue,
Dafydd reproves his eyes'
Impetuous falconry
About the kneeling girl.
Stones to the walls fly back,
The gay manors are full
Of music; the poets return
To feed at the royal tables.
Who dreams of failure now
That the oak woods are loud
With the last hurrying feet
Seeking the English plain?

Expatriates

Not British; certainly
Not English. Welsh
With all the associations,
Black hair and black heart
Under a smooth skin
Sallow as vellum; sharp
Of bone and wit that is turned
As a knife against us.
Four centuries now
We have been leaving
The hills and the high moors
For the jewelled pavements
Easing our veins of their dark peat
By slow transfusions.
In the drab streets
That never knew
The cold stream's sibilants
Our tongues are coated with
A dustier speech.
With the year's passing
We have forgotten
The far lakes,
Aled and Eiddwen, whose blue litmus
Alone could detect
The mind's acid.

Hyddgen

The place, Hyddgen;
The time, the fifth
Century since Glyn Dŵr
Was here with his men.
He beat the English.
Does it matter now
In the rain? The English
Don't want to come:
Summer country.
The Welsh, too:
A barren victory?
Look at those sheep,
On such small bones
The best mutton,
But not for him,
The hireling shepherd.
History goes on;
On the rock the lichen
Records it: no mention
Of them, of us.

A Line from St. David's

I am sending you this letter,
Something for neo-Edwardians
Of a test-tube age to grow glum about
In their conditioned libraries.
As I came here by way of Plwmp,
There were hawkweeds in the hedges;
Nature had invested all her gold
In the industry of the soil.
There were larks, too, like a fresh chorus
Of dew, and I thought, remembering Dewi
The water-drinker, the way back
Is not so far as the way forward.
Here the cathedral's bubble of stone
Is still unpricked by the mind's needle,
And the wall lettuce in the crevices
Is as green now as when Giraldus
Altered the colour of his thought
By drinking from the Welsh fountain...

I ramble; what I wanted to say
Was that the day has a blue lining
Partly of sky, partly of sea;
That the old currents are in the grass,
Though rust has becalmed the plough.
Somewhere a man sharpens a scythe;
A child watches him from the brink
Of his own speech, and this is of more
Importance than all the visitors keeping
A spry saint asleep in his tomb.

Welsh

Why must I write so?
I'm Welsh, see:
A real Cymro,
Peat in my veins.
I was born late;
She claimed me,
Brought me up nice,
No hardship;
Only the one loss,
I can't speak my own
Language — Iesu,
All those good words;
And I outside them,
Picking up alms
From blonde strangers.
I don't like their talk,
Their split vowels;
Names that are ghosts
From a green era.
I want my own
Speech, to be made
Free of its terms,
I want the right word
For the gut's trouble,
When I see this land
With its farms empty
Of folk, and the stone
Manuscripts blurring
In wind and rain.
I want the town even,
The open door
Framing a slut,
So she can speak Welsh
And bear children
To accuse the womb
That bore me.

Afforestation

It's a population of trees
Colonising the old
Haunts of men; I prefer,
Listening to their talk,
The bare language of grass
To what the woods say,
Standing in black crowds
Under the stars at night
Or in the sun's way.
The grass feeds the sheep;
The sheep give the wool
For warm clothing, but these — ?
I see the cheap times
Against which they grow:
Thin houses for dupes,
Pages of pale trash,
A world that has gone sour
With spruce. Cut them down,
They won't take the weight
Of any of the strong bodies
For which the wind sighs.

Welcome

You can come in.
You can come a long way;
We can't stop you.
You can come up the roads
Or by railway;
You can land from the air.
You can walk this country
From end to end;
But you won't be inside;
You must stop at the bar,
The old bar of speech.

We have learnt your own
Language, but don't
Let it take you in;
It's not what you mean,
It's what you pay with
Everywhere you go,
Pleased at the price
In shop windows.
There is no way there;
Past town and factory
You must travel back
To the cold bud of water
In the hard rock.

A Country

At fifty he was still trying to deceive
Himself. He went out at night,
Imagining the dark country
Between the border and the coast
Was still Wales; the old language
Came to him on the wind's lips;
There were intimations of farms
Whose calendar was a green hill.

And yet under such skies the land
Had no more right to its name
Than a corpse had; self-given wounds
Wasted it. It lay like a bone
Thrown aside and of no use
For anything except shame to gnaw.

A Lecturer

A little man,
Sallow,
Keeping close to the wall
Of life; his quick smile
Of recognition a cure
For loneliness; he'll take you
Any time on a tour
Of the Welsh language, its flowering
While yours was clay soil.

It seeds in him.
Fitfully,
As the mood blows, poetry
In this small plot
Of manhood opens
Its rich petals; the smell
Is familiar. Watch him,
As with short steps he goes.
Not dangerous?
He has been in gaol.

The Patriot

He had that rare gift that what he said,
Even the simplest statement, could inflame
The mind and heart of the hearer. Those who saw
For the first time that small figure
With the Welsh words leaving his lips
As quietly as doves on an errand
Of peace-making, could not imagine
The fierceness of their huge entry
At the ear's porch.
                                   And when he wrote,
Drawing the ink from his own veins'
Blood and iron, the sentences
Opened again the concealed wounds
Of history in the comfortable flesh.

Looking at Sheep

Yes, I know. They are like primroses;
Their ears are the colour of the stems
Of primroses; and their eyes --
Two halves of a nut.
                     But images
Like this are for sheer fancy
To play with. Seeing how Wales fares
Now, I will attend rather
To things as they are: to green grass
That is not ours; to visitors
Buying us up. Thousands of mouths
Are emptying their waste speech
About us, and an Elsan culture
Threatens us.
                What would they say
Who bled here, warriors
Of a free people? Savagely
On castles they were the sole cause
Of, the sun still goes down red.

Hafod Lom

Hafod Lom, the poor holding:
I have become used to its
Beauty, the ornamentation
Of its bare walls with grey
And gold lichen; to its chimney
Tasselled with grasses. Outside
In the ruined orchard the leaves
Are richer than fruit; music
From a solitary robin plays
Like a small fountain. It is hard
To recall here the drabness
Of past lives, who wore their days
Raggedly, seeking meaning
In a lean rib. Imagine a child's
Upbringing, who took for truth
That rough acreage the rain
Fenced; who sowed his dreams
Hopelessly in the wind blowing
Off bare plates. Yet often from such
Those men came, who, through windows
In the thick mist peering down
To the low country, saw learning
Ready to reap. Their long gnawing
At life's crust gave them teeth
And a strong jaw and perseverance
For the mastication of the fact.

The Provincial

He is that dark side
Of you that you keep
Hidden, the poor relation
You avoid. Since you left
The villages' and the fields'
Mire, you have looked
Forward only at your reflection
In plastics. Do you never
Pause thoughtful before the trash
Of windows, and on scenes
Of false snow see bleakness
Of the real world impose
His figure, who is native
Of such truth, and makes his way
With dignity to the same
Poor, cold, bare
Resting place as do you
With your immense solvency for show?

A Welshman at St. James' Park

I am invited to enter these gardens
As one of the public, and to conduct myself
In accordance with the regulations;
To keep off the grass and sample flowers
Without touching them; to admire birds
That have been seduced from wildness by
Bread they are pelted with.
                   I am not one
Of the public; I have come a long way
To realise it. Under the sun's
Feathers are the sinews of stone,
The curved claws.
                   I think of a Welsh hill
That is without fencing, and the men,
Bosworth blind, who left the heather
And the high pastures of the heart. I fumble
In the pocket's emptiness; my ticket
Was in two pieces. I kept half.

Schoonermen

Great in this,
They made small ships do
Big things, leaping hurdles
Of the stiff sea, horse against horses
in the tide race.
What has Rio
To do with Pwllheli? Ask winds
Bitter as ever
With their black shag. Ask the quays
Stained with spittle.
Four days out
With bad cargo
Fever took the crew;
The mate and boatswain,
Peering in turn
Through the spray's window,
Brought her home. Memory aches
In the bones' rigging. If tales were tall,
Waves were taller.
From long years
In a salt school, caned by brine,
They came landward
With the eyes of boys,
The Welsh accent
Thick in their sails.

Sir Gelli Meurig

(Elizabethan)

I imagine it, a land
Rain-soaked, far away
In the west, in time;
The sea folded too rough
On the shingle, with hard
Breakers and steep
To climb; but game-ridden
And lining his small table
Too thickly — Gelli Meurig,
Squire of a few
Acres, but swollen-headed
With dreaming of a return
To incense, to the confections
Of worship; a Welsh fly
Caught in a web spun
For a hornet.
        Don't blame him.
Others have turned their backs,
As he did, and do so still,
On our land. Leaves light
The autumn, but not for them.
Emptily the sea's cradle
Rocks. They want the town
And its baubles; the fine clothes
They dress one in, who manage
The strings. Helplessly they dance
To a mad tune, who at home
In the bracken could have remained
Humble but free.

Traeth Maelgwn

Blue sea; clouds coming up
For convention only; the marks
On the sand, that mean nothing
And don't have to to the fat,
Monoglot stranger. Maelgwn
Was here once, juggling
With the sea; there were rulers
In Wales then, men jealous
Of her honour. He put down
Rivals, made himself king
Of the waves, too; his throne
Buoyant — that rocking beacon
Its image. He kept his power
By intelligence; we lose
Ours for lack of it,
Holding our caps out
Beside a framed view
We never painted, counting
The few casual cowries
With which we are fobbed off.

Llanrhaeadr-ym-Mochnant

This is where he sought God.
And found him? The centuries
Have been content to follow
Down passages of serene prose.

There is no portrait of him
But in the gallery of
The imagination: a brow
With the hair's feathers
Spilled on it? A cheek
Too hollow? Rows of teeth
Broken on the unmanageable bone

Of language? In this small room
By the river expiating the sin .
Of his namesake?
              The smooth words
Over which his mind flowed
Have become an heirloom. Beauty
Is how you say it, and the truth,
Like this mountain-born torrent,
Is content to hurry
Not too furiously by.

Resort

The sea flicks its spray over it.
Occasionally a high tide
Swills its cellars. For the rest
There are only the few streets
With the boredom of their windows.
People, people: the erect species
With its restlessness and the need to pay —
What have they come here to find?
Must they return to the vomit
Of the factories? On the conveyor belt
Of their interests they circle the town
To emerge jaded at the pier;
To look at the water with dull eyes
Resentfully, not understanding
A syllable. Did they expect
The sea, too, to be bi-lingual?

Welcome to Wales

Come to Wales
To be buried; the undertaker
Will arrange it for you. We have
The sites and a long line
Of clients going back
To the first milkman who watered
His honour. How they endow
Our country with their polished
Memorials! No one lives
In our villages, but they dream
Of returning from the rigours
Of the pound's climate. Why not
Try it? We can always raise
Some mourners, and the amens
Are ready. This is what
Chapels are for; their varnish
Wears well and will go
With most coffins. Let us
Quote you; our terms
Are the lowest, and we offer,
Dirt cheap, a place where
It is lovely to lie.

Loyalties

The prince walks upon the carpet
Our hearts have unrolled
For him; a worn carpet,
I fear. We are a poor
People; we should have saved up
For this; these rents, these blood stains,
This erosion of the edges
Of it, do him no honour.

And where does it lead to
Anyway? About the table
The shopkeepers are all attention.
I would have run it to the door
Of the holding where Puw lived
Once, wrapping the language
About him, watching the trickle
Of his children down the hill's side.

Alma Mater

Cardiff to some is
capital is port crouched
on Tâf incubating
the cobbles that will turn
gold is a bright string
of beads that the dark
wears an arena
for triumphs a pint
pays for is the nation's
museum the burial ground
of its speech a gallery
of bought faces to me is
streets houses one
where a girl relieved herself
of me is a stone
doorstep I played
on a while in a brief
ignorance of where I belonged

Toast

I look at Wales now forty
years on. Was there a chance,
as some hoped, that maggots,
burrowing in its carcase, would grow
wings and take themselves off,
leaving at least the bones to acquire
a finish? The opposite happened.
The stench, travelling on the wind
out of the west, was the lure for more
flies, befouling our winding-sheet
with their droppings. What shall I say
to a people to whom provincialism
is a reasonable asking-price
for survival? I salute your
astuteness and drink to your future
from a wine-glass brimming with acid rain.

Drowning

They were irreplaceable and forgettable,
inhabitants of the parish and speakers
of the Welsh tongue. I looked on and
there was one less and one less and one less.

They were not of the soil, but contributed
to it in dying, a manure not
to be referred to as such, but from which
poetry is grown and legends and green tales.

Their immortality was what they hoped for
by being kind. Their smiles were such as,
exercised so often, became perennial
as flowers, blossoming where they had been cut down.

I ministered uneasily among them until
what had been gaps in the straggling hedgerow
of the nation widened to reveal the emptiness
that was inside, where echoes haunted and thin ghosts.

A rare place, but one identifiable
with other places where on as deep a sea
men have clung to the last spars of their language
and gone down with it, unremembered but uncomplaining.

Gwalia

Here there is holy water,
old stone and a sky
that is timeless. Let them be.

Here are a slow people
with drained hearts, offering
a welcome to those who can pay.

Here is the glass peace
the pilgrims once travelled toward
that the aircraft make brittle.

Here the last Welshman's cry
has shrunk to an echo indistinguishable
from silence: Stranger, go home.

The Parlour

To time's pre-paid
telegram no answer.
Beyond Offa's Dyke
the media betray us.

You knock with the wrong
tongue. Between you
and our kitchen the front room
with our framed casualties

in your fool wars. Over
polite tea we hand you
the iced cake of translation.
It is not what we mean.

Welsh Village

There was a window
    I stood by
in a Welsh village,
myself looking in and he
out, the framed soldier,
waiting for the return
    home never to be.

I was along again,
no — was it last week?
    not only the soldier
gone, but the house gone, too.

Welshman's Epitaph

Had a country, renounced
it. Drove his course on
by the star in the east.
Arrived finding

the machine in the manger;
not one of the three
gifts he presented
restored to him but the myrrh.

A Land

Their souls are something smaller
        than the mountain above them
and give them more trouble.
             They are not touched
either by the sun rising at morning
or the sun setting at evening.
             They are all in shadow
pale and winding themselves about each other
            inhibiting growth.

Death lives in this village, the ambulance plies
             back and fore,
and they look at it through the eternal downpour
        of their tears.
             Who was it found
truth's pebble in the stripling
        river? No-one believed him.

They have hard hands that money adheres
          to like the scales
of some hideous disease, so that they grizzle
as it is picked off. And the chapel crouches,
a stone monster, waiting to spring,
waiting with the disinfectant of its language
           for the bodies rotting with
their unsaid prayers.
         It is at such times
that they sing, not music
         so much as the sound of a nation
rending itself, fierce with all the promise
        of a beauty that might have been theirs.

Saunders Lewis

And he dared them;
Dared them to grow old and bitter
As he. He kept his pen clean
By burying it in their fat
Flesh. He was ascetic and Wales
His diet. He lived off the harsh fare
Of her troubles, worn yet heady
At moments with the poets' wine.

A recluse, then; himself
His hermitage? Unhabited
He moved among us; would have led
To rebellion. Small as he was
He towered, the trigger of his mind
Cocked, ready to let fly with his scorn.

The Cause

Time does not forgive
the vanquished. Will eternity
forgive? And without memory
there, how shall we ask?

I was for peace, and heard the words
of Shakespeare's Harry
on Crispin's Day sing in my veins –
for a poor cause. For what better

cause let them haul down
our language, or fly it
at half-mast at the funeral
of our self-respect? Christian

we would have matched them
cheek for cheek. For unbelievers
in our existence is there even
that much of our face to save?

Dic Aberdaron

Telling us so much
it so much the more
withholds. Who was he?
The clothes a labourer's

clothes: coarse trousers, torn
jacket, a mole-skin
cap. But that volume
under the arm — a

hedge-poet, a scholar
by rushlight? We look
closer: no soil in
that eye, but light

generated by a
mind charging itself
at its own sources.
Radiant soul, shrugging

the type's ignorance
off, he hastens towards
us, to the future
we inhabit and must

welcome him to, but
nervously, all too
aware of the discrepancy
with his expectations.

Dead Worthies

Where is our poetry
but in the footnotes?
What laurels for famous
men but asterisks and numbers?

Branwen (Refer below).
Llywelyn — there is but
one, eternally on his way
to an assignation.

Morgan, no pirate,
emptying his treasure
from buccaneering
among the vocabulary. Ann,

handmaid of the Lord,
giving herself to the
Bridegroom, still virgin.
Williams Parry, quarrying

his cynghanedd among
Bethesda slate in
the twilight of the language.
Lloyd George, not David,

William, who in defence
of what his brother
had abandoned, made a case
out of staying at home.

Waiting

Here are mountains to ascend
not to preach from,
not to summon one's disciples
to, but to see far off the dream that is life:
winged yachts hovering over
a gentian sea; sun–making
windscreens; the human torrent
irrigating tunefully the waste places.

Ah, Jerusalem, Jerusalem!
Is it for nothing our chapels were christened
with Hebrew names? The Book rusts
in the empty pulpits above empty
pews, but the Word ticks inside
remorselessly as the bomb that is timed soon to go off.

Deprivation

All this beauty,
and all the pain
of beholding it emptied
of a people who were not worthy of it.
It is the morning of a world
become suddenly evening.
There was never any noon here.
Noon is an absence of shadow,
the stillness of contemplation,
of a balance achieved
between light and dark.
When they were born,
they began to die to the view
that has been taken from them
by others. Over their sour
tea they talk of a time
they thought they were alive.
God, in this light this
country is a brittle
instrument laid on one side
by one people, taken up
by another to play their twanged
accompaniment upon it, to which
the birds of Rhiannon
are refusing to sing.

Fugue for Ann Griffiths

In which period
    do you get lost?
The roads lead
    under a twentieth century
sky to the peace
    of the nineteenth. There it is,
as she left it,
    too small to be chrysalis
of that clenched soul.
    Under the eaves the martins
continue her singing.
    Down this path she set off
for the earlier dancing
    of the body; but under the myrtle
the Bridegroom was waiting
    for her on her way home.

To put it differently
yet the same, listen,
friend:
    A nineteenth century
                calm;
that is, a countryside
    not fenced in
by cables and pylons,
but open to thought to blow in
    from as near as may be
to the truth.
        There were evenings
she would break it. See her
    at the dance, round
and round, hand
    in hand, weaving
invisible threads. When
you are young... But
    there was One
with his eye on her;

                she saw him stand
under the branches.
                History insists
on a marriage, but the husband was as cuckolded
as Joseph.
                Listen again:

        To the knocker at the door:
        'Miss Thomas has gone dancing.'

        To the caller in time:
        'The mistress is sitting the dance

        out with God at her side.'
        To the traveller up learning's

        slope: 'She is ahead of you on her knees.
        She who had decomposed

        is composed again in her hymns.
        The dust settles on the Welsh language,

        but is blown away in great gusts
        week by week in chapel after chapel.'

Is there a scholarship that grows
naturally as the lichen? How
did she, a daughter of the land, come
by her learning? You have seen
her face, figure-head of a ship
outward bound? But she was not
alone; a trinity of persons
saw to it she kept on course
like one apprenticed since early
days to the difficulty of navigation
in rough seas. She described her turbulence
to her confessor, who was the more

astonished at the fathoms
of anguish over which she had
attained to the calmness of her harbours.

There are other pilgrimages
    to make beside Jerusalem, Rome;
beside the one into the no-man's-
    land beyond the microscope's carry.

If you came in winter,
    you would find the tree
with your belief still crucified
    upon it, that for her at all

times was in blossom, the resurrection
    of one that had come seminally
down to raise the deciduous human
    body to the condition of his body.

Hostilities were other peoples'.
Though a prisoner of the Lord
she was taken without fighting.

That was in the peace before
the wars that were to end
war. If there was a campaign

for her countrymen, it was one
against sin. Musically
they were conscripted to proclaim

Sunday after Sunday the year
round they were on God's side. England
meanwhile detected its enemies

from afar. These made friends
out in the fields because
of its halo with the ancestral scarecrow.

Has she waited all these years
for me to forget myself
and do her homage? I begin
now: Ann Thomas, Ann Griffiths,
one of a thousand Anns chosen
to confound your parentage
with your culture — I know
Powys, the leafy backwaters
it is easy for the spirit to forget
its destiny in and put on soil
for its crown. You walked solitary
there and were not tempted,
or took your temptation as calling
to see Christ rising in April
out of that same soil and clothing
his nakedness like a tree. Your similes
were agricultural and profound.
As winter is forgiven by spring's
blossom, so defoliated man,
thrusting his sick hand in the earth's
side is redeemed by conviction.
Ann, dear, what can our scholarship
do but wander like Efyrnwy
your grass library, wondering at the absence
of all volumes but one? The question
teases us like the undying
echo of an Amen high up
in the cumulus rafters over Dolanog.

The theologians disagree
on their priorities. For her
the centuries' rhetoric contracted
to the three-letter word. What was sin
but the felix culpa enabling
a daughter of the soil to move
in divine circles? This was before

53

the bomb, before the annihilation
of six million Jews. It appears now
the confession of a child before
an upholstered knee; her achievement
the sensitising of the Welsh
conscience to the English rebuke.
The contemporary miracle is the feeding
of the multitude on the sublime
mushroom, while the Jesus,
who was her lover, is a face
gathering moss on the gable
of a defunct chapel, a myth shifting
its place to the wrong end
of the spectrum under the Doppler
effect of the recession of our belief.

Three pilgrimages to Bardsey
equalling one to Rome — How close
need a shrine be to be too far
for the traveller of to-day who is in
a hurry? Spare an hour or two
for Dolanog — no stone cross,
no Holy Father. What question
has the country to ask, looking as if
nothing has happened since the earth
cooled? And what is your question?
She was young and was taken.
If one asked you: 'Are you glad
to have been born?' would you let
the positivist reply for you
by putting your car in gear, or watch
the exuberance of nature in a lost
village, that is life saying Amen
to itself? Here for a few years
the spirit sang on a bone bough
at eternity's window, the flesh trembling

at the splendour of a forgiveness
too impossible to believe in, yet believing.

Are the Amens over? Ann (Gymraeg)
you have gone now but left us with the question
that has a child's simplicity and a child's depth:
Does the one who called to you,

when the tree was green, call us
also, if with changed voice,
now the leaves have fallen and the boughs
are of plastic, to the same thing?

        She listened to him.
        We listen to her.
        She was in time
        chosen. We but infer
        from the union of time
        with space the possibility
        of survival. She who was born
        first must be overtaken
        by our to-morrow.
        So with wings pinned
        and fuel rationed,
        let us put on speed
        to remain still
        through the dark hours
        in which prayer gathers
        on the brow like dew,
        where at dawn the footprints
        of one who invisibly
        but so close passed
        discover a direction.

_____

Other R.S. Thomas Titles

Critical Writings on R.S. Thomas
Edited by Sandra Anstey

A revised and expanded second edition of this popular book updates its survey of the critical response to Thomas's work up to *Counterpoint*, published in 1990. The seven new essayists include Tony Brown, John Barnie, James A. Davies, and Tony Bianchi, who join earlier authorities Roland Mathias, R. George Thomas and Brian Morris. It also includes an invaluable and extensive bibliography of critical material on R.S. Thomas.

> "This volume is a welcome handbook to the work of one of the most distinguished living poets." — Raymond Garlick

pp. 236   1-85411-062-4   Hardback £12.95

The Page's Drift: R.S. Thomas at Eighty
Edited by M. Wynn Thomas

A specially commissioned collection of essays to celebrate the achievement of R.S. Thomas as he reaches his eightieth birthday in 1993. The book's themes range from the hill farmer persona of Iago Prytherch to his response to visual art, from a comparison with Dylan Thomas to his unsteady relations with God, from the autobiographical element in his work to the significance of the sea. Contributors include Anne Stevenson, Helen Vendler, Marie-Térèse Castay, Walford Davies and Ned Thomas. Plus poems by R.S. Thomas and Gillian Clarke, and a select bibliography. A book not to be missed.

pp.232   1-85411-093-4   hbk £19.95   1-85411-100-0   pbk £8.95